Songs in the Night

Adele Pilkington

Onwards and Upwards Publishers
Berkeley House, 11 Nightingale Crescent, Leatherhead, Surrey, KT24 6PD.
www.onwardsandupwards.org

Printed in the UK.

ISBN: 978-1-907509-71-1

Graphic design: Leah-Maarit

Endorsements

Adele Pilkington's love for God shines through in these verses. As she expresses her awe at creation and concern for this world, she shares that love with us, lifts us up out of ourselves and points us towards His great goodness.

Marion L.S. Carson
Author, Lecturer

I sincerely commend this heart-warming new composition of original verse penned with refreshing candour and colour. These pages are living letters of rich encouragement and uplift for times like these. Each verse encourages us to look up and beyond our present troubles to the One from whom our help comes, and will provide for many who read them songs for our darkest nights. Written from a wide subject interest and with a warmth readers will feel, the author has provided us with a truly inspirational read.

Dr Alec Passmore
Evangelist, Pastor, Bible Teacher

I would like to dedicate this collection of poems to my Mum whose quiet and sure faith has been a daily encouragement. Also, to the many who have been good and faithful companions on the journey of life.

To those, such as my Dad, who now rejoice in Christ's nearer presence and others who journey on, my heartfelt thanks for the pricelessness and joy of Christian fellowship.

Contents

sites.google.com/site/**adelespoetry**

Prologue

Whilst reading and writing poetry is something I have enjoyed from an early age, I have often found that inspiration comes in moments of stillness, when the world is sleeping and when we can be most at one with God.

My choice for the title of this collection of poems also reflects God's faithfulness through life's difficulties. Whilst life may not turn out the way we hope and whilst some of our most cherished dreams my remain unfulfilled, we can find a deep joy in knowing Jesus as our Lord and Saviour, which enables us to praise Him even in the darkest moments.

Isaiah 30:29 (NIV)

And you will sing
as on the night you celebrate a holy festival;
your hearts will rejoice
as when people playing pipes go up
to the mountain of the LORD,
to the Rock of Israel.

All Creation Sings

Matthew 6:26

Look at the birds of the air; they do not sow or reap or store away in barns, and yet your heavenly Father feeds them. Are you not much more valuable than they?

Introduction

I have always marvelled at the vast diversity of creation, each creature so individually designed to be adapted to their varied environments. As each season passes their needs are provided for by the One who is able to meet our every need. In the words of one of my favourite hymns, "Something lives in every hue Christless eyes have never seen."[1] God's care for His creation is constant and shows His enduring love for us all.

[1] 'Loved with everlasting love', George W Robinson (1838-1877)

Be Still

The wonder of a sunset, its colours bright ablaze
Warms a summer evening, creates a gentle haze.
The glory of a rainbow which lights a sky of grey,
Heralding good things as storm clouds drift away.
The beauty of a rose in bloom, its softness and its scent,
Moonlight catches glistening stars amid the firmament.
The majesty of birds in flight, lifted high 'mid skies of blue,
The splendour of a towering tree, touched by the morning dew.
The blessing of a field of grain, gold against the sun,
The promise of provision before our work's begun.
Each captures our attention, and in our stillness we reflect,
Every facet is a miracle of creation that's perfect.
So much achieved without our aid, so much in our lives too,
"Be still and know that I am God,"[2] He says,
Be still and let God work His miracles in you.

---

[2] Psalm 46:10

Change

Summer green to autumn gold –
Again the colours blend;
The falling leaves, the crispy air,
Another season's end.
The sheaves of wheat and orchard fruit,
Swelled by the summer rain,
Add colour to the changing scene
As harvest comes again.
Long hazy days of summer
Give way to misty nights,
As swifts and swallows take to wing,
Begin their yearly flight.
And soon another season
Is drawing to a close;
The rosy shades of autumn
Are lost in winter snows.

Clouds

Soft billows of perfect white
Drifting on high against the blue;
How wonderful to stand and gaze
At such a panoramic view.

From day to day a changing pattern
Heralding a shower of rain,
Casting bolts of angry thunder,
Then reveal the sun again.

Birds fly higher, try to catch you,
Find the secret of your form;
Winds are blowing, how you've altered,
Streaming, swirling, now you're gone.

Country Thoughts

Swirling winds and rushing water,
Endless lanes of leafy green,
'Neath each twig and rosy garland,
Safe from man – a world unseen.
Up above 'mid clouds of wonder,
Soar with graceful wings on high,
Birds whose plumage casts a rainbow
Fleetingly across the sky.
Oh, to feel the soft wind blowing,
Oh, to hear this fanfare cry –
Worshipping their One Creator,
Watching o'er His work on high.
Let me stand and watch a moment,
Hold this joy within my heart,
Loving, keeping all He gives me,
In this world, to play my part.

Fledglings

Little sparrow, I can see you,
High above me in your nest –
Ever trying, dreams of flying,
Tired wings have earned a rest.
All your every need provided,
Daily warmth and food and love,
Helpless though you seem, your safety
Is assured by God above.
He can see your every movement,
He will catch you if you fall;
Such a tiny life, yet precious
To God who hears our every call.
In your life, I see mine mirrored,
I too need a helping hand,
Lifted up by One who loves me,
My Father always understands.

Gull

A freedom that no man can know,
I'm the master of all I survey,
And I glide and drift along,
As my wings catch the gold of the day.
Here solitude describes existence,
And dreams are a way to survive;
My eyes can appreciate wonder
That surrounds and is full of life.
My kingdom is sky and ocean,
The clouds and the rocks my home,
The sun and the rain sustain me
As I bob over rippling foam.
Though we have no crowns and glory,
Though we have no silver and gold,
We are part of life's wonderful story
And a part that will never grow old.
Caressed by the sun in the morning,
And lulled by the waves at night,
The path of our flight is directed
By a powerful, guiding Light.

Hidden Powers

From such a tiny seed, perfumed flower will show;
From such a tiny acorn, a mighty oak will grow.
From such a downy chick, a graceful bird soars high;
From such a cloudy morning, a bright sun lights the sky.
From such a gentle stream, a river rushes through,
And tiny stars above light up the midnight blue.
Each little breeze that whispers can stir the mighty trees;
Each little raindrop falling can flood the open seas.
Each miracle to cherish is sent from God above,
Shows power which knows no limits, and never-ending love.

Morning Star

Across the midnight mantle
A thousand shimmering eyes
Penetrate the deepest darkness
With precious beams of light.

Like jewels in a cluster
On the finest regal crown,
They glitter in the heavens
Giving light to all around.

Even on the darkest night
They shine as bright as day,
Their light a message to the world
To all who hope and pray.

For though the world is dark in sin,
The morning star will shine
Within the hearts of all who know
His gift of love divine.

Until that glorious day shall dawn
When brightness fills the skies,
The awesome glory of the Lord
Our Dayspring from on high.

The conqueror of sin and death
Is the conqueror of night.
He reigns supreme upon His throne;
He is Our eternal light.

Adele Pilkington

Refreshment

Sun-kissed crystals now cascading
Across the cloudless sky of blue,
Each one fashioned for its purpose,
Refreshing, bringing life anew;
Softly falling down from heaven,
Lifted by the gentle breeze,
Cushioned by the sun-scorched gardens,
Welcomed by the yearning trees.
Thirst is quenched and strength renewed,
Colours shimmer, bright aflame,
Nature drinks life-giving waters,
Thankful for each drop of rain.

Retirement

Down in a corner by a shady tree,
Lost in the joy of a dream,
Caressed by the warmth of the golden sun,
Her eyes bear an arrogant gleam.
For Bess has seen many a glorious day,
When her prowess and grace were renowned;
Now she gallops and leaps o'er the fences of time
As she lies on the soft grass of home.

Home is a meadow with stream and with trees,
Away from the bustle of town;
Alone and forgotten her dark eyes still shine,
As she thinks of the joy she has known.
Her coat, it is dull, and her mane so unkempt,
Now that garlands and rosettes have gone;
Yet remembers a time when old bones were young,
And she galloped and gambolled along.

Time has erased the memories of those
Who once rode and kept her with pride,
So she lives with her thoughts and the birds as her friends
Now that glory and conquest have died.

Adele Pilkington

The Beauty of Barrenness

O Lord and our Creator
Of this vastness that surrounds,
Though alone I feel your presence,
Though I cannot hear a sound,
In the beauty of this stillness
A joy just fills my heart,
That amidst this awesome wonder
My life still plays a part.
A God whose hands set stars in space,
Whose hands have shaped the vast cliff face,
Who owns, controls all I can see,
Can care for such a one as me.
It seems in such a barren place
No life could grow or thrive,
Yet God's provisions are all around
If we will seek and find.
So, if trouble comes or life seems bleak
Our Lord has things in hand.
There's beauty in the wilderness;
It's part of His great plan.

A Desert Paintbox

Majestic peaks of rosy granite,
Sun-kissed 'neath a sky of blue,
Softly cast a lengthening shadow,
Browns and golds of every hue.
High above a bird is flying,
Soaring high on glistening wing;
Not a sound to break the stillness –
Yet the host of nature sings.
Here and there a burst of colour
Add a contrast to this scene,
Delicate lilac, white and yellows,
Sun-parched soil and little green.
Each deft touch the Master Painter
Has designed to play its part.
So majestic, catch the stillness,
Hold it dear within your heart.

A Song of Love Unknown

John 17:3 (NIV)

Now this is eternal life: that they know you, the only true God, and Jesus Christ, whom you have sent.

Introduction

I can honestly say that I am always humbled by the indisputable fact that the Son of God willingly chose to lay down His life for me and that this would be true if I was the only human being who had ever lived. When considering position and status in human terms, my life is of little account, and I would certainly not be guaranteed an audience with the rulers and sovereigns of this world. However, I have access to the King of Kings and Lord of Lords at any time and the guaranteed peace of His presence – a reality which causes the human heart to sing.

The Comforter

"I'll never leave you nor forsake you"[3] –
This His promise ever true.
"With My Father now abiding,
I'll send my Comforter to you."

Always with us, ever present
Since Pentecost of Bible times –
A rushing wind and tongues of fire,
Filling hearts and changing lives.

Men prophesying, seeing visions,
Old rejoicing, dreaming dreams,
Wise men baffled by this presence,
Can't comprehend just what it means.

Bringing gifts and fruit a-plenty
Through our lives to show a sign,
This indwelling Holy Spirit
Is a gift of love divine.

Not a one-day happening,
Lost in time, a well-worn story;
No, the Holy Spirit will remain,
Until our Lord returns in glory.

---

[3] Based on Hebrews 13:5

The Cost of Trust

How much does it cost you to follow the Lord,
To follow the way He has planned,
To walk in obedience, trusting in Him,
Placing your life in His hands?

How much does it cost a mother to give
A child she has yearned for so long
In service to others, obeying God's will,
Never questioning to whom he belongs?

How much does it cost a young child to leave
Those that he cherishes dear,
To walk in God's way and trust in His word,
Without doubt, or envy or fear?

God's plan and purpose are one day revealed,
How crucial their roles in it all.
If we still desire God's blessings to flow
We must trust and obey when He calls.

An Evening Prayer

As we come to the end of another day
And reflect on all that has gone,
The love and support that has come our way,
The friends who have helped us along,
The peace that has dwelt in our hearts again,
Safe and secure in His love,
So before we enter a land of dreams
Let's remember our Father above.
Let's thank Him for things 'day to day',
And for each passing year,
For home and work and family,
For all we hold so dear.
Let's thank Him for His every gift
With love so freely given,
And pray that we may someday rest
With our Father up in heaven.

The Gift and the Giver

Grace is a gift which is given to one
Undeserving, unworthy to claim,
A gift of eternal life and rebirth,
By calling our Lord's precious name.

Mercy is receiving what we didn't deserve,
Freedom when punishment's due,
Justice demanding a penalty paid,
But mercy is love breaking through.

For the love sent from God I cannot express
By my own simple word or tongue;
It's a love that demands that I give my whole self
For His service and purpose – lifelong.

A love which can melt our hearts and our fears,
Which draws us once more to His side,
No more condemnation, our Hope is the Lord,
In His truth we'll forever abide.

An Invitation

There was no room in the inn that night,
When God incarnate came
To a people in bondage and darkness;
Was His mission to be in vain?

There was no place in that time for Him.
Though Conqueror, He came not to fight;
His Word was His sword, His truth a shield,
The gift of salvation, His might.

There seemed no place in a world for Him
That knew only hate and fear,
Where 'power', 'wealth' and 'position' were
The words people wanted to hear.

There seemed no place for the message He brought
Of humility, love and grace,
And yet His Word cries out to us still –
In your hearts can you find a place?

Can you find a place for the One who died,
Shed His blood to pay for your sin?
He is knocking on the door of your heart;
Sinner, won't you let Him in?

For He who dwells in glory above,
The Ruler of time and space,
Willingly enters and reigns within;
In my heart He has found a place.

My All in All

My friend, He is my friend,
Through all life's battles
Unto the journey's end.

My guide, He is my guide,
A beacon in the wilderness,
A shelter safe to hide.

My life, He is my life,
His loving arms surrounding me
Will keep me safe eternally.

My Lord, you are My Lord,
I'll serve you all my days,
And may my heart forever sing,
An endless hymn of praise.

Adele Pilkington

Name Above All Names

God of heaven, O Most Holy,
Came to earth in manger lowly.

King of Kings, enthroned in splendour,
Came a baby, gentle, tender.

Lion of Judah, not in might
Came to earth that still calm night.

Our Saviour, bringing eternal life,
Came 'mid poverty and strife.

Lord of Lords, our hearts adore you;
Lowly babe we bow before you.

Prince of peace, our lives we bring,
To lay before you, Heavenly King.

No Greater Love

Love I can never comprehend,
So great God's love for me,
Who sent His only Son to die
On lonely Calvary.

Love which knows no limits,
Whose patience never ends.
Love which through life's journey
Upholds, supports, defends.

Love whose source is boundless,
Grace so rich and free,
A God of righteous justice,
Yet so merciful to me.

Love which never counts the cost,
Which floods the sinner's soul,
Washing clean our every stain,
Restoring, making whole.

Love that's given all to us
Demands that we should live,
In sure and certain hope of
The salvation that He gives.

We must uphold His Word, His truth,
Before the laws of men,
Saved by His grace to follow Him,
Until He returns again.

Until He returns to take us home
To dwell with Him above,
Then we shall come to fully know
The depth of God's great love.

Adele Pilkington

Prayerfulness

Prayer is not just spoken.
It's heartfelt thought and need.
It's praise and adoration,
The will to intercede.

It's taking time to be with God,
To honour Him alone,
To bring our burdens and our cares
And lay them at His throne.

It's fellowship that's made in heaven;
It's closeness to our Lord,
Resting in His loving care
And feeding on His word.

It's the uttering of thankful hearts
When words cannot convey,
And quiet confession for the times
We've stumbled on our way.

It's lifting up each other's needs
And knowing we are heard,
And claiming from the promises
God gives us in His word.

It's prayer that draws us near to God.
Though problems may assail us,
He hears and answers every prayer;
Our Lord will never fail us.

Redemption Day

Arms stretched out, prepared to die,
Reach out in love to me;
Hands which suffered cruel nails
Caress me lovingly.

Eyes which saw the jeering crowd,
Who made the blind to see,
Watch me now from heaven above
And guide me tenderly.

Your broken body knows my pain,
No grief you cannot quell;
You suffered hurt, my sin and shame,
You broke the gates of hell.

No power on earth could halt God's plan
Or hold you on that tree;
You came to die but rose again
And set the captives free.

You came, my ransomed soul to claim,
My worth to me so small,
And yet for me you bled and died;
Your love has conquered all.

Your love has touched my heart, O Lord;
I need you every hour,
Filled by your Holy Spirit, Lord,
Enabled by Your power.

To uphold by word and prayer
The Kingdom you will bring,
Until I see you face to face,
My Saviour, Lord and King.

Victory

He is risen; Christ is risen.
Jesus rolled the stone away –
All the powers of darkness vanquished;
Death no longer holds its sway.

Satan conquered, God triumphant,
All the host of nature sings;
In our hearts enthroned forever,
Jesus, our Lord, our Life, our King.

He knows our weaknesses and failures,
Feels our pain, our hurt, our need,
Sits at God's right hand in heaven;
For each one He intercedes.

Lord, our lives we lay before you;
All our praise to you we bring.
Lord in heaven, how we adore you,
Risen Saviour, Risen King.

Whose Life is it Anyway?

Not I that live but You that live in me,
Dear Lord, this is my fervent prayer.
Let no pride in me be found;
Let my life reflect Your love;
Let my words resound Your praise;
Let my acts reflect Your ways.
As a servant may I find...
Your love – there is no greater kind.

Companions on the Journey

Hebrews 13:5-6 (NIV)

God has said, "Never will I leave you; never will I forsake you."
So we say with confidence, "The Lord is my helper;
I will not be afraid. What can mere mortals do to me?"

Introduction

Life is a much richer experience as a consequence of those we meet along our way, whether family, friends or those who seem to be chance encounters but can often have significant impact on shaping the people we grow to be. Even those encounters which prove more challenging, and on which we do not look back with undiluted pleasure, have an important place to play in the Master's plan which directs all our paths, whether or not we care to acknowledge this. His grace is always available for each moment.

Adele Pilkington

Angels

Life is full of special people,
Guardian angels close at hand.
So many times we just don't see them;
How oft' we fail to understand.

In our trials and tribulations,
Not alone to struggle on;
Always there just when we need them,
Giving help and then they're gone.

Who can tell when we might need them?
Who can tell where they might be?
Unsuspected individuals
Always watching over me.

So remember guardian angels,
Sent to minister and care
By the One who loves us dearly,
On a wing and on a prayer.

Keeper of the Light

The Keeper of the lighthouse beam
Looks out into a world, unseen
By fishermen with meagre sail,
Who 'gainst the driving winds prevail,
Steering carefully round the brink,
Lest unseen rocks their vessels sink;
Whilst tossed about 'mid towering waves,
That guiding light their vessel saves.
The lantern's beam still glowing bright
Will penetrate the darkest night,
And keep the boat safe on its course,
To see that none should suffer loss,
But fishermen must follow near,
The source of light which guides them here.

Marriage Vows

A cosy fire, a comfy chair,
A hand stretched out to say, "I care."
A friendly hug, a kindly word,
A problem shared, a trouble heard,
A look that says, "It's quite ok;
I know just how you feel today."
Time to share our doubts and fears,
To share the laughter and the tears.
A presence when we're most alone,
Comfort that is 'home from home'.
A look that means, "That's not the way;
Is that really what you meant to say?"
A word of wisdom carefully planned,
Unseen support, a helping hand,
Companionship that's sealed for life,
The friendship between man and wife.

A Miracle

Here I am though none can see me
Safe within a cushioned home;
Months of planning, hoping, praying,
Just a week and yet I've grown.

Such a miracle to witness
From the seed of man and wife,
This a blessed act of union,
From this love there springs new life.

Deep within, my heart is beating,
Though I am still very small,
How can anybody question,
"Is this really life at all?"

How I feel my father's presence!
How I love my mother's voice!
Calming waters all around me –
This my life and this my choice.

Now I know they feel my movement,
How I love to feel their touch!
Only halfway there – yet perfect;
I resemble them so much!

With each day I grow I'm certain
I am a gift from God above;
By my life and by my presence
I reflect our Father's love.

Now the time is fast approaching
Through the miracle of birth.
Let me show those many doubters
What my tiny life is worth.

Adele Pilkington

On Passing a Stranger

Of glories unspoken, of stories untold,
He carries the morals of a world that's grown old.
With his fading apparel but boots shining bright,
He may not be so nimble but still knows what's right.
As he sees the injustice and troubled affairs
Of the folk who forget him or don't seem to care,
The love of his life still burns in his heart,
Though time and the grave have kept them apart.
He treasures the memories of things that have gone;
The medals he fought for are all that he owns.
His body is tiring as life nears its end,
But people ignore him, he's nobody's friend.
They seem to forget that once he was young,
His heart full of pride and his muscles so strong,
So look for the wisdom behind this disguise;
Learn from this man – it may be a surprise.

Nurture

A tiny human form arrives
Transforming homes and changing lives;
Despite this outward frail form,
An independent spirit born.

Yet needing love and strength to grow,
Security, someone to show
How to walk, and talk and run,
Provision when the hard work's done.

But within this frame of loving care,
Learning how to give and share,
To meet the needs of others too,
As those who do their best for you.

Learning trust, respect and truth,
Established firmly in our youth,
That growing we might in our turn
Teach the truth that we have learned.

This truth is hidden in God's word –
A message now too seldom heard –
As people learn to take, not give,
Consider less how others live.

What we sow, we will reap one day;
Lord, keep us in the narrow way,
For a life of 'self' can never be
The life that you have planned for me.

Special Friends

Special friends are gifts from God.
Their worth no man can measure;
Their value can't be matched against
The world's most costly treasure.
A friend to share your hopes and care,
To lift you up through times of prayer,
To share your laughter, meet a need,
Encourage, strengthen, intercede;
But the greatest blessing surely comes
When two spirits meet as one,
Lifted to a higher plain
Than earthly friendship can sustain.
No barriers of age and time
Can thwart the union of heart and mind,
Sharing in a greater love,
God's Word, His glory, heaven above,
His love, which from on high descends,
Reflected in such special friends.

Special People

Who decides what's right and wrong?
Who can know where treasure lies?
Within a stunted human frame,
A living spirit in disguise.

What potential trapped within
Lips that utter not a word;
Limbs that limp and lifeless lie
Cannot make their meaning heard.

Eyes no blinding light can touch,
Darkness meets both day and night,
Bodies writhing helplessly –
Is it just themselves they fight?

Are these greater handicaps
Than heads that turn away in fear,
Or ignorance and prejudice,
Unwilling ears that will not hear?

Because in finite human terms
A life does not fulfil 'the norm',
What right have we to pick and choose
Who can or can't be born?

God's grace falls upon each life,
Blessing in some unique form.
His love to such we cannot know;
They communicate with Him alone.

Can we reach out and touch these lives
In some simple, gentle way,
And meet a need that words alone
Of splendid speech cannot convey?

Each life is precious in His sight,
Each a purpose in His plan,
None more precious than another
In the fellowship of God and man.

The Lifeboat

Towering winds and crashing torrents,
Threatening skies of dismal grey,
Tossed about 'mid seas of fury,
The harbour light seems far away.

The tiny vessel valiantly struggles
To find a sailor lost, alone.
Hope burns high in hearts of loved ones;
Each harbour light invites them home.

Selfless service drives them onward,
Unwavering in their torrid quest;
Menacing winds and angry thunder –
Will their vessel stand the test?

A cry for help, they struggle onwards,
Each sinew straining in the fight;
Strength is tested to the limit
To answer someone else's plight.

A man aboard, a life preserved,
How great the cost, how rich the gain;
Home to comforts, hearts rejoicing,
Their mission hasn't been in vain.

Adele Pilkington

Tranquillity

Can you ever find peace
In a world full of trouble,
A Harbour to anchor
Steadfast in a storm,
Where no one is striving,
Or dealing, conniving,
Where love and contentment
Can both find a home?

Where you may find friendship
That lasts for a lifetime,
A promise of comfort,
Support on the way,
A place where the sunshine
Lights up every morning,
And joy fills your heart
Till the end of the day?

This place lies within you;
Each person may find it,
If they hold in their heart
What they know to be true,
For the Lord will bestow
To each one who receives Him
A soul that is free,
And a life that is new.

Reflections

What can you see in the eyes of a child –
A world of adventure, a magic carpet ride?
Where time has no meaning
And dreams can all come true,
Where happiness is living
And learning all things new.

The puzzled expression that comes with the teens,
A search for self and meaning,
A shattering of dreams.
Expressions of defiance, yet childlike helplessness,
Lead on to self-assurance or angry bitterness;
Within the frame of adulthood
With schedules to keep,
Careers are carefully moulded
'Mid success or harsh defeat.

Yet, tender eyes that watch her child
Hope that time will never pass,
Cling onto prams and baby ways
That seem to go so fast.

Eyes now dim and clouded
With many passing years,
Have seen life's little pitfalls,
The laughter and the tears.
So much to tell, so little time,
It seems to be that way,
But hope lives on; those eyes might see
The dawn of a new day.

With Love to Mum and Dad

The joy of a home and a family
Are gifts beyond all measure;
The loving arms of a mum and dad
Are the world's greatest treasure.
For no one else would spend the years
Of time, care and devotion,
And no one else's heart would break
Or be filled with such emotion.
From nappies, toys and baby things
To bruised knees, school and wedding rings.
They listen when others turn away,
They protect from the knocks of every day,
They love and care against the song
Of "I know best; it's you that's wrong."
They help us grow, be wise and learn
To be good parents in our turn.

THROUGH ALL THE CHANGING SCENES OF LIFE

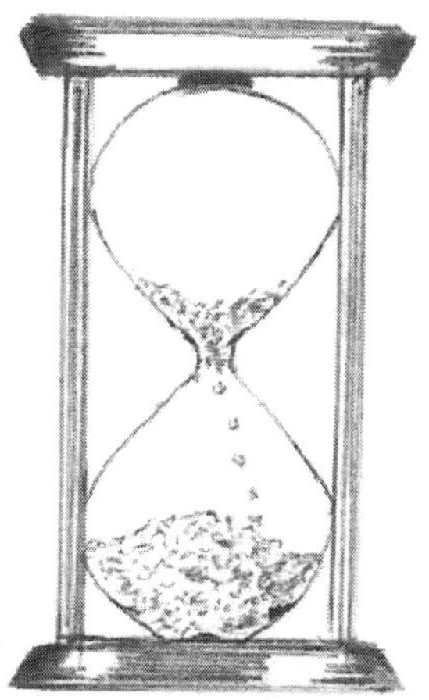

Luke 21:28 (NIV)

When these things begin to take place, stand up and lift up your heads, because your redemption is drawing near.

Introduction

There can be no doubt that we live in extraordinary days and are witnessing events on a global scale which have not been seen to the same extent in previous generations. The frequency with which 'natural' disasters have occurred in the recent decades is on an unprecedented scale. Scientists, whilst making strides in many areas, seem to have no answers to the changing climate which threatens future generations. Financial markets remain volatile, and global governments struggle to achieve an equitable balance. Do we see these events as mere happenstance or is there a more significant and deeper spiritual explanation?

Adele Pilkington

Creation Matters

How on earth can mortal man
Assume to know our Master's plan?
How indeed can we presume
That life evolves 'beyond the moon'?
Our lives are short;
We're here, we're gone.
God's purposes
Go ever on.

We had no say in when we came,
Or where we might be born.
We did not choose our family,
Our culture or our home.
Whilst we might feel in control
Of our lives from day to day,
Can we stop the sun from rising,
Or chase the rain away?
Can we stop each passing season,
Or the hours from ticking by?
Can we stop the sun from setting,
Or hold it in the sky?
Can we change one day a year from now?
Or when our life is done,
Can we hope to go on living
By earthly powers alone?

Only God has all the answers –
He knows from whence we came;
He knows where we are going
If we've trusted in His name.
He's our King and our Creator;
Everything is in His hands.
When earthly powers have crumbled
Our Lord's still in command.

Eternity Secured

Little by little we grow older each day,
Moment by moment life passes away,
The splendour of youth loses its shine,
Age reaps its effects with the passage of time.
Yet we have a hope of new life and new birth,
An eternal existence on leaving this earth –
New hearts and new voices, and new songs to sing,
A home made in heaven to reign with a King,
Where limbs won't grow weary despite passing years,
All suffering ended, no sorrow or tears.
If Christ is our Saviour, Redeemer and Lord,
We can dwell here on earth secure in His Word.
By dying to self and living in Him,
By admitting our need and confessing our sin,
Death and the grave are no longer the end;
There's new life and a purpose which Christ did intend,
To serve and praise our Saviour for all eternity,
In love and peace abiding, in perfect unity.

Adele Pilkington

Faith in the Future

As the old year passes with its joys and with its sorrows,
And we face a new unknown, another fresh tomorrow,
Let's not dwell upon our failures, or the deeds of yesterday;
Let's lay them down at Jesus' feet, as we kneel to humbly pray.
For our sins when once forgiven are forgotten for all time;
The slate's wiped clean, its only guilt that troubles still our mind.
It's not our Lord's intent that we should live with old regrets,
For the God who loves us dearly, He forgives and He forgets,
And only asks we leave our future firmly in His hands –
All our tomorrows shaped and purposed by our Master's plan.
Let God lead you by His light, and you will find the road before you
Leads on with Him to victory and everlasting glory.

Heavenly Treasure

Do we place our trust in politics, or princes or philosophers?
Does our future lie in finance or the forecast of astrologers?
Are stocks and shares an anchor, the hope on which we rest?
Will our planning for the future really stand the test?
Is security the world can offer ever safe at all,
As walls of nations tumble and politicians fall?
Do we have a sure foundation that will stand the test of time,
Or will doubts and fears assail us if our fortunes fast decline?
If our life and health are threatened, will everything be lost?
By faith in Christ alone can we know a perfect trust;
Our future guaranteed and eternity secured,
To those investing in our heavenly Father's treasure store.

Look Up

As storm clouds gather round us,
And the path ahead seems drear,
Let us heed the signs and warnings:
The Day of the Lord draws near.
Whilst philosophers search for answers,
And fools still dig for gold,
Whilst empires crumble round us,
True saints of God are bold.
For with their vision skywards,
They await the shout and call;
When Christ's redeemed are raptured,
He will gather one and all.
Let's not waste the days before us,
But seek God's will and plan,
To offer whilst we are able
The Bread of Life to dying man.

The Master Plan

Life is such a rich tapestry
Of changing patterns and scenes,
Of things well planned, considered,
And wild and foolish schemes.
A mix of colours blending,
In their weave can we detect
Those flaws beneath the surface,
That this 'perfect' scheme reflects.
Within each separate portion,
Loose threads, unfinished ends
May spoil the finished product
If we do not make amends.
So let the weaving follow
A greater plan than we
Can ever fashion for ourselves –
That finest tapestry.

Promises

Promises, promises!
How often do we find
The things we really meant to do
Have somehow slipped our mind?
Do our hearts reflect our words
Or is this fickle thought?
Do we really mean to do
The things we know we ought?
Let's be glad God's promises
Unlike ours will never fail;
The Word of God omnipotent
Eternally prevails.

Quiet Times

It's often in the quiet times
When you most touch my heart,
The times we leave the world behind
And set ourselves apart;
Those times of rest and solitude,
When our hearts with Yours are one,
When we take the time to think, reflect,
On all that You have done.

The wonders of creation,
Your power and majesty,
Yet loving us You sent your Son
To die at Calvary.

So amidst the noise, confusion
Of our erstwhile, earthly days,
May we know the quiet confidence
That's ensured each time we pray.
May we know our life is fashioned
By a greater power above;
No power on earth can separate us
From our Father's love.

What God promised on that hillside,
In another time and place
Will remain alive within our hearts,
'Til our eyes see Jesus' face.

A Prayer for Awakening

O Lord, I pray your Spirit like a mighty wind would blow
On the people of our nation, to let your power show.
Like a wave that keeps on rolling, like a never ending tide,
Filling hearts to overflowing, changing minds and changing lives;
Like a stream whose source is endless, to supply their every need,
Bringing life to all it touches, washing clean from sin and greed.
Rushing onward through the nations, may it grow from year to year,
Opening eyes once blind to see, unstopping ears to hear.
May it heal the lives of many who have suffered hate and blame,
May its source unite all people to worship Jesus' name.
Within the hearts of all You love, may your Holy Spirit bring
A never-ending hymn of praise to You our heavenly King.

Sustainability

All the news is death and warfare,
Killing man and men's ideals,
Strife and anger, hurt and violence –
Is this all that now appeals?
We have created all this turmoil,
Humankind with no-one's aid,
'Progress' of our worldly nations;
What a dreadful mess we've made!

People starving, children dying,
A world so steeped in pride and sin,
People crying, should be searching
For a cause from deep within.
For this world is 'Satan's playground' –
Famine, bloodshed, war, disease –
This the price of our wrongdoing,
All results which he achieves.

Yet we all should know the answer
To our quest to save the earth;
It lies within a single mission
That began with Jesus' birth,
In His life of humble service,
Death which cleansed our sins away;
All He asks is that we serve Him,
Give our lives to Him today.

For our God shall be our juror;
All this world is His estate.
We must repent of pride and evil,
Through Jesus Christ our advocate.

Adele Pilkington

Twenty-first Century Trials

Broken homes and broken lives;
Broken dreams that youth inspired;
Violence, mayhem, petty crime;
Disordered lives, disillusioned minds;
No rhyme or reason, hope or trust;
Ideals trampled into dust;
Grim tenements blotting out the sky;
Another promise – another lie?
What future where foundations fail:
A 'hope in hell' or life in jail?
No nurturing of thought or will,
No heart so cold that love can't fill.
Yet life is cheap – small price to pay
And one less mouth to feed today;
Another family 'gone to pot',
And none prepared to stop the rot.
No protest or half-hearted prayer
Will lift this mantle of despair,
No cries of "Justice, peace for all!"
A nation blinded, as darkness falls.

Tribulation

The world goes on searching for peace in our time.
Though storm clouds are gathering, we heed not the signs;
Men searching for cures for the ills of our race
Cannot see before them the troubles we face.
In a nation where power and wealth are the goals,
Have we no burden for the loss of men's souls?
Men seeking an end to global pollution,
Don't realise there's a final solution –
That financial problems we find ourselves in
All find their root in the question of sin.
No matter how great the statesman or nation,
The answers aren't found by negotiation.
No matter what science's advances may boast
They don't yield the answers we're needing the most.
For the truth we are seeking is found in God's Word,
A message today seldom heeded or heard.
Yet God's Kingdom will come, and soon we will find
The answer to peace that's so troubled mankind,
But in knowing our Lord we have peace from the start;
He's established the Kingdom of Peace in our hearts.

OUR FAITHFUL GOD

Jeremiah 31:37 (NIV)

This is what the LORD says: "Only if the heavens above can be measured and the foundations of the earth below be searched out will I reject all the descendants of Israel because of all they have done," declares the LORD.

Introduction

The focus of world media attention so often centres on the Middle East and the tiny nation of Israel. Given this nation is approximately the size of Wales, it seems implausible that it should maintain such global interest. What is perhaps most remarkable is the debate about this nation's right to exist. God has made clear through His Word His purposes and plans for Israel which, as the changing scenes of life continue to unfold, will become all the more apparent. Despite humankind's desire to determine the history of this nation, we can look forward with confidence to the time when through them all nations of the earth will be blessed (Genesis 12:3).

Chosen Land

A field full of flowers,
A hill topped with snow,
A desert so barren
Where cacti grow,
A valley of fruit trees,
A rocky cliff face,
They're part of the contrast
Of God's chosen place.
Dusty dry summers
Yet winters of rain,
A man on his donkey
O'er rugged terrain,
A wandering nomad,
A barefooted child –
Worlds apart from the city
(Yet just a few miles)
With hotels, apartments,
And Western ideals,
Where power and position
Have gained most appeal,
Where culture, religion
Cause moral divides,
In a land where God's blessing
Forever resides.
But one day all people united will stand,
And peace will return to this beautiful land.

Fishers of Men

A life transformed, so Peter thought,
A simple fisherman.
He fished to feed his family;
God had another plan.
They heard the call and followed Him,
Though many doubted them;
He taught them truths, how they might be
Fishers amongst men.
He came to reach the lowly ones,
The humble and the meek,
To reach them by His power and love,
And let His kingdom speak.
He asked that they His path might tread;
They could not comprehend
That a life of fame and favour
He never did intend.
They watched Him die upon a tree,
Their Lord and Master lost.
They saw His love for all mankind;
They learned what love could cost.
Their hopes renewed, their Master risen,
He was not to remain,
But He would guide them in His paths
Till He returned again.
So they followed on His narrow path;
They dared His truth to speak.
Now we must follow in their steps,
Till we His kingdom reach.

Adele Pilkington

Harvest of a Nation

We watch your early rains, O Lord,
Prepare the fallow ground,
Break up the hardness, barrenness,
Of all that now surrounds.
We pray that rain will come in time,
Will cover all the ground,
Sufficient for the present time,
Sent by our Father's hand.
The almond tree begins to bloom,
We know that spring is near;
We pray your latter rains, O Lord,
Abundant fall this year.
We pray that seeds which dormant lay
Will one day yield much grain;
The vine in blossom, fig in fruit,
Swelled by your latter rain.
We pray the rain and sun in turn
Bring grain, and oil, and wine –
A Harvest like none other
From the keeper of the Vine.

Holy City

Jerusalem – how that name thrills me,
City of old, yet promises new,
Chosen from all the world's great nations,
Fashioned by God, whose word is truth.
City of history, long you have suffered,
Fought for and longed for by many men,
Shattered by heavy battle and conquests,
Desolate ruins – and yet you remain!
Even 'in spirit' when reality failed you,
Deep in the hearts of those you love,
Still today you stand divided...
Yet greater plans await above.
One day the destiny of all men
Will rise again within your walls;
That day eternity will greet you,
O city of gold and marble halls.
Our Lord will reign in mighty justice,
Your walls resound with hymns of praise,
Your misery and wars forgotten,
A heavenly city of endless days.

Land of Contrast

A patchwork quilt of new spring flowers
Covers a hillside lush and green;
So close, but seems so far away
From drying heat and desert scene.
Within the corner of the world,
It seems that God once had a plan
To choose a land and call it 'home' –
His goal since first the world began.
He filled it with a race of people
From every corner of the earth –
A mix of culture and religion,
Yet share a common root and birth.
A mix of race, of tongue and status,
So like the land to which they came,
A mix of every colour blending;
No two places look the same.
From snow-capped peaks to coral beaches,
And cedars in a forest glen,
This land of contrasts God created
To challenge the hearts of men.

Missed Opportunity?

How God can work such miracles
In lives of humble men –
A fisher and a tax man,
And those whom men condemn?
Through simple faith and trust in God,
We see a life transform,
Through the work of God above –
New life, new spirit born,
Prepared to die and serve their Lord,
To suffer scorn and shame,
A poor and lowly life on earth,
Yet 'kings' when born again.
We should, through such example,
Search our lives for chances lost;
Are we prepared to serve our Lord,
And never count the cost?

A Mother's Love

"And a sword shall pierce your heart..."[4]
But how could those words convey
The pain and anguish she felt
As she witnessed events that day?

As she cradled His body cold and still,
She thought of the angel's voice;
"Blessed amongst women"[5] she truly had been,
But this was His will and her choice.

The scent of the myrrh, so clearly a part
Of the message the wise men brought.
The child she had loved and nurtured was gone;
The bitterness saddened her heart.

She thought of her own life – such a small role,
This handmaiden of the Lord.
She surely would die in His place if she could;
Her heart felt the pain of that sword.

She knew that her Saviour, her Master and Lord,
Was also her son and her friend;
She knew that His mission was purposed and planned
But never knew how it would end.

As they led her away from that cold, lonely tomb,
Her mind filled with doubt and dismay;
Her heart dared to think of a heavenly home
Where she'd meet Him again someday.

---

[4] Luke 2:35
[5] Luke 1:42

Arising the third day, she went to that place,
Yet He wasn't there; He had risen.
'Midst tears, new joy flooded her heart,
Realising the hope she'd been given.

The angels, the shepherds, the wise men and sage –
She now understood God's plan:
Eternal redemption. How blessed she had been
In knowing the Son of Man.

Adele Pilkington

Of Ritual and Religion

A misty stillness pervades the morning air;
The minaret is calling Allah's faithful to prayer.
Across the busy city by the Western Wall,
The frenzied prayer of men with Talmud and with shawl.
A city small and compact, emotions at a peak,
So many ideologies, thoughts and voices speak.
Man with men in conflict over ritual and land,
Yet church, mosque and synagogue side by side still stand.
God longs for hearts united, for peace within this place,
As brother stands with brother, and our eyes see Jesus' face,
No longer war and conflict, no longer hate and blame;
Minds enlightened, lives inspired, worshipping His name.

The Olive Tree

The Olive tree, its bark so gnarled,
Has watched the passing years,
The blistering sun, the driving rain,
The hardships and the tears.
Its roots so strong, though pulled away,
Grow deep on rocky ground;
No tree quite like the Olive
Has ever since been found.
Its branches will not take the graft
Of any other tree;
Its fruit in season, holy oil,
Preserve identity.
Though battered by the storms of life,
New shoots spring from the earth,
Restoring life eternally,
A symbol of new birth.
Its produce brings both food and light
To refresh the weary soul.
O Lord, as grafts divinely laid,
May we fulfil our role.
May we value the root and stem;
May we uphold this truth
That on the day our Lord returns
The world will share its fruit.

Adele Pilkington

A Prayer for Israel

Please pray for Israel,
For peace in that place,
For love between brother,
No hatred of race.

Please pray for Israel,
Its beauty so rare,
A land full of promise,
The whole world might share.

Don't weep for Israel,
For it is God's plan,
From this race would rise
The salvation of man.

Please pray, as one day,
The Bible foretold,
Our Lord will return
To its city of gold.

And nation by nation
Will know of it when
Jesus reigns in glory,
In Jerusalem.

Persecution

How can it be we let them suffer?
How can it be we let them die?
A nation lost in mindless bloodshed;
I hear those little children cry.

Cold and hungry, lost and lonely,
No parents now to comfort them,
Haunted nights in icy barracks –
How could we these lives condemn?

Stripped of all their pride, possessions,
Humiliated to the grave –
This the fate of God's own nation,
No attempt their lives to save.

Yellow stars and cruel jeering,
Hunted for their race and name,
Flashback to a page in history;
The story always sounds the same.

Why is it that the Jewish nation
Has been the scapegoat for our hate?
Is God alone their only refuge?
None of them deserves this fate.

For our Lord is of their number;
Such a wondrous gift He gave.
Through his death, His pain and suffering,
We can live beyond the grave.

We should love God's chosen people,
Hold them dear in thought and prayer;
Then our lives reflect God's pleasure
When we show we really care.

Adele Pilkington

Shephelah

A rainbow of vibrant colours fills the eager eye,
Gentle rolling hillsides, soft against the sky.

Birds of every colour, sweet their voices raise,
Plant and shrub their leaves extend, join in joyful praise.

Tall and lofty cedars, almond tree in bloom,
Heavy laden citrus, unruly white broom.
Poppy, daisy, cyclamen, and anemone,
Their perfume and their colour, a perfect symphony.

They speak of their Creator, His wonder and His love,
A world so full of beauty, a gift from God above.

Epilogue

It is my hope that the contents of this book will bring encouragement to those who read it and enable them to grow in their journey of faith.

In taking the time to commit these items to print, I also hope that they will provide a more enduring legacy. Whilst I have not been blessed by having children of my own I have been privileged to have the opportunity to support others who provide education and humanitarian support to underprivileged children in a number of locations across the world. My hope is that these and similar projects continue to flourish in the future.

In this regard it is intended that 100% of the royalties which may arise from the sale of this book will be distributed evenly among the following children's charities:

- Education Sponsorship for India's Dalit children
  www.freeadalitchild.org
- Orphan's Tear – A ministry of Heaven's Family
  www.orphanstear.org.uk
- Tikva Orphans Programme
  www.4922trust.org
- World Share Child Aid
  www.worldshare.org.uk

- Adele Pilkington -

Micah 6:8 (NIV)
And what does the LORD require of you?
To act justly and to love mercy
and to walk humbly with your God.

Index